POCKET POWER

BECOME THE PERSON YOU WERE BORN TO BE

RUDIE JAKERSON

Filbert
Publishing

Copyright © 2018 by Filbert Publishing

All rights reserved.

No part of this book may be reproduced in any form or by any electronic or mechanical means, including information storage and retrieval systems, without written permission from the author, except for the use of brief quotations in a book review.

Get your hands on awesome resources to fuel your creative life by heading to http://FilbertPublshing.com and subscribing to Writing Etc., the zine that'll make your project sparkle, help you market smart, and thrive. :)

This is for every dreamer, to every hopeless romantic who dared to foster ambition, then set it aside when reality wouldn't cooperate.
All is not lost.
This book is for every fearless soul who stubbornly battles impossible odds to become the person they always knew they could be.
It's for the adventurer, the crazy artist, anyone who proudly wears rose colored glasses because they know with all their heart, they'll someday make it to their ultimate goal... to Polaris... and beyond.

YOUR INVITATION

Before you get too deep into Pocket POWER, I'd like to extend a special invitation for you to become a member of our little Pocket POWER community. This online group is dedicated to helping you not only streamline your POWER practice, it's completely devoted to helping you remain inspired, hopeful, and able to build your dream life on your own terms.

This isn't your typical "think positive and grow rich" set up. Nope. We're firmly grounded in reality, success oriented, and most certainly *not* a "pitch fest" continually trying to sell you something or another.

So yeah... if you're craving meaty information with just a side of fluff (after all, who can live without a little of that?) join us. If I do say so myself, we're a hoot.

Here's the link:

http://PocketPowerBooks.com

Oh... and did I mention your private membership is free? We don't offer this to every Tom, Dick, and Sally. Only people serious about reclaiming their ultimate goal are invited to check out this somewhat secret web page.

So, what are you waiting for? You've got nothing to lose, everything to gain…

CONTENTS

Introduction ix

1. How to Become What You Were Born to Be 1
2. The Birth of Pocket Power 5
3. The Pocket Power Philosophy 9
4. P is for POW 13
5. O is for Own Your Time 18
6. W is for Win the Mindset Game 23
7. E is for Empathy 27
8. R is for Review and Relax 32
9. Putting it All Together 36
10. Toolbox to Transform Your Life 41
11. The 30 Second Challenge 48
12. A Bonus! 52

About the Author 53

INTRODUCTION

How to Use this Information to Thrive

I think I'm an anomaly of nature. Every time I read a book about success, the majority of the time, I'm told if I only maintain a sunny disposition, if I think happy thoughts, if I steadfastly ignore all evidence to the contrary, success beyond my wildest dreams is mine.

I have a minor problem with that.

If I allow just one peek at reality, which to be honest, can be rather difficult to ignore, I plainly see with my own two eyes that every single successful person I know didn't ignore reality, they didn't sit around all day dreaming, continually thinking happy thoughts. In fact, they actually got down in the trenches and did stuff. They worked. They planned. They watched for trends. They kept an eye on any and all competition.

In other words, they generally utilized down and dirty, based in reality, hard-core techniques to navigate and maintain their businesses.

Telling folks hoping to improve their situation to merely

think happy thoughts, dream, and focus solely on what you want without any concrete tools to achieve that goal is (in my opinion) not only ineffective, it's a special kind of arrogance.

Sure, mindset is one facet of success. I'll give you that one. But without actual tools, easy techniques, a guide to alter the trajectory of your life... achieving your ultimate goal is much more difficult.

I don't know about you, but I'm done with mixing a ton of woo with success. That's so last decade, back when The Secret flew to the top of the bestseller list, creating an army of dreamers who visualized success, chanted empty (often unbelievable) affirmations, seminar hopped, then were told they did something incorrect when money didn't magically fall from the sky.

Don't get me wrong. Dreams definitely come true, for sure. However, what they didn't tell you is that the only people who achieved long term financial success in that scenario were the marketers promising success minus actual reality based strategies to get there.

I feel bad when good people are duped into investing hundreds, sometimes thousands, of dollars on half baked schemes doomed to fail. But, it continues.

Just today, I received yet another email from a guru who claims to have cured his cancer through positive thinking. It's been a whole month since he completed his grueling "allopathic" treatments, he has no idea what his future holds (I've dealt with cancer), but nope... it was his great attitude that cleared his scans.

Another email arrived, this one promising that if I just meditated for another five minutes a day, each moment would get better than the last. I couldn't help but wonder, with this exponential happiness flowing into my life, at what point would I be so happy that my body simply couldn't take anymore?

Here's the deal (IMHO): Life is pretty awesome. So, why can't I look at reality? No matter what your dreams of success are, you're going to have to contend with lots of real situations erupting all around you.

Happiness is awesome. But, you're not going to be happy every day. If that were the case, if happiness became your default position, how would you be able to recognize that you were happy?

It's the full palette of colors that allows you to see the beauty in any situation. It's the dark hues of sadness that allow you to enjoy the bright shades of happiness. You love deeper after a mind numbing loss.

Many of societies most beautiful works of art grapple with the negative sides of life. Songs of love and loss dominate the pop charts. Entire libraries have been created celebrating death. The fear of not achieving one's full potential drives many entrepreneurs forward.

See my point? Don't fear the negative. Instead, how about you use its power to propel your efforts forward?

After all, you're going to experience the entire rainbow of emotions in this lifetime. And that's a good thing.

And as you make your way through this powerful little book, just realize every technique is based in reality. So, from here on in, you have my explicit permission to feel your emotions, every single one of them, good and bad, high and low, every color you can imagine.

After all, emotions are one of the key elements that makes you human. And it's that humanness that makes you truly unique.

Are you ready? Go ahead, feel good. Make plans. Dream. These are all good things.

Also, feel bad when it's appropriate. You might even want to cry on occasion. Allow someone awesome to break your heart, then rebuild yourself into something stronger.

And in the meantime, enjoy this little book. It's a fun, simple, reality based toolbox designed to help you achieve whatever it is you need or want.

Are you ready to get cracking?

Let's go.

1
HOW TO BECOME WHAT YOU WERE BORN TO BE

Let's talk about patterns.

A pattern is a repeated thought process that triggers a behavior. Until you think about it, you probably aren't aware of the myriad of patterns that infiltrate, and control, your life.

In fact your life is downright ruled by patterns. Everything you do, is governed by unconscious actions, behaviors you may not even be aware of, many of which are completely invisible (until you make an effort to unveil them), and terribly useful.

Unfortunately, some of these unconscious behaviors, patterns, may not suit your needs in the way they once did.

Let me give you an example of what I'm talking about:

When you wake up in the morning, you probably have a routine. This is what I do: I like to get up, make my bed, take out the dog, check email, eat breakfast. That's a routine, pattern, that works for me. I want to run through my morning as efficiently as possible (thought) and that thought triggers this repeating behavior every morning.

That's an example of a pattern that works.

However, as I've matured, grown up, some of the patterns from my youth haven't aged as well. For example, when confronted with a difficult situation, my first impulse is to consume foods that don't align with my desire to maintain a healthy body. If the phone rings and I notice it's someone I don't want to talk to, it's really weird how I find my feet traipsing towards the kitchen before I even begin the conversation. It wasn't until my jeans became painfully tight that I realized how destructive that pattern had become.

In a nutshell, my tendency (pattern) to eat through my problems clashed with my very important goal to keep my body healthy.

Here's another example:

In my family of origin, it was considered bad form to criticize, speak ill of anyone, anytime. So, when a situation went amok, I always made sure I could find a way to assign blame to myself. I wasn't fast enough, smart enough, I didn't communicate well enough... no matter the scenario, blame always landed squarely on my shoulders.

Although I often didn't understand how I could be responsible for circumstances beyond my control, it was always safer to blame myself, engage in the requisite mental whipping, and simply live a perfect life. That pattern worked well until I married and interactions with others became a little more complicated.

With so many situations beyond my personal control, I spent far too many years mentally berating myself for being unable to control every outcome of every situation. And when the "Law of Attraction," which states you and you alone are responsible for everything that happens in your life, became a popular mantra, I hopped on that familiar horse hoping that if I simply kept a perky attitude, I could somehow control the actions of everyone around me, the outcome of every situation, and feel good as wonderful things exploded around me.

It didn't exactly unfold that way. Every time actions beyond my control affected my life in a negative way, I found myself blaming myself. The more I blamed myself, the more I felt like a failure. The more I felt like a failure, the more I realized how worthless my life had become.

It was a downward spiral, a pattern that clearly didn't suit my needs.

It wasn't until I broke that pattern, accepted that I cannot take the blame for anyone's actions beyond my own, the realization that I cannot and will not try to control everything, once that pattern no longer governed my life, I discovered true freedom to become the person I really wanted to be... the person I felt I was born to be.

Discovering your own patterns sometimes feels like a game of wack-a-mole. About the time you figure you're in a pretty good space, boom... another puzzling pattern pops its head into your consciousness and you get to gaze upon its (sometimes) odd glory as it silently, for better or worse, rules your life.

And that's the whole point of this book: You need to identify your patterns, determine if they serve you, and live with the new knowledge confronting that pattern grants you.

As you identify and reckon with these wily patterns, you will gain incredible insight into the person you actually are versus the person you've always wanted to be. It's an amazing journey, one that I hope you'll enjoy. It's self exploration at its finest and most pure.

I hope you'll approach this adventure with an open heart and with tremendous compassion. If you've noticed you've been engaging in patterns that don't serve you, don't create a new pattern of debasing yourself for behaviors you weren't aware of.

Patterns are a normal facet of mental health. Without them, humankind wouldn't have survived. It's only when those patterns no longer serve you that it's time to dismantle the old and create new ones.

And that's exactly what we're going to do, starting today, this very moment.

When you monitor and modify your recurring patterns, it's only a matter of time before you start catching glimpses of the person you always knew you were. And after that, you'll discover that with very little effort, you'll actually transform into that person.

You'll achieve goals you never thought possible. You'll meet people you never dreamed you'd meet. You'll find yourself places you never thought possible.

But most of all, you'll like yourself. You'll truly believe anything is possible. And you'll feel like you have a hand in your own destiny.

Are you ready to begin?

2

THE BIRTH OF POCKET POWER

I'd just received a cancer diagnosis. Talk about a kick in the teeth. It was totally unexpected, out of the blue. In fact, I've never heard anybody say, 'Yup. Totally saw that coming..."

But, then something worse happened.

But, I'm getting ahead of myself. Time to back up a little.

I've always known I was going to be a writer. Even in third grade, I continually wove tales, entrancing my elementary school friends. Writing, to me, is as natural as breathing.

I once knew a songwriter who called spinning words a "curse" because as difficult as his job was, the only occupation more difficult was any job that didn't allow him to write.

It's just in our blood, this need to convey understanding, help others, construct amazing worlds.

So, after my cancer diagnosis, the unimaginable happened: words left me. I could no longer write. My imagination was blank as the plains of Minnesota.

Like a row of dominoes, everything that was important

in my life, tumbled. Crumbled into a pile of nothingness. A tremendous chunk of what I thought was "me" vanished.

I scrambled to keep semblance of a business life, after all, I was the owner of a successful publishing company, but everything felt hollow as I sailed on the waves of my past successes, towards a future I didn't understand. I felt like a fraud, a carpenter without a hammer, a musician without his instrument.

I searched high and low for an answer to my problem, my inability to write.

I tried positive thinking. "I'm a competent writer," I'd repeat, "nothing can stop me."

But truth was, something stopped me. And try as I might, I couldn't figure out what that something was.

The positive thinking track left me feeling inadequate as I, for some reason, found myself unable to create the life of my dreams by mere thought alone. I realized that while a good attitude is probably a good thing, that train of thinking lacked something very important: a concrete plan of action, something, a physical action, I could do to help me progress towards my ultimate goal and help me write again.

I considered professional counseling. However, it turned out my insurance wouldn't pay. Plus, I wasn't entirely positive I wanted that pre-existing condition on my medical record when I wasn't entirely positive my situation was permanent.

I searched for solution through prayer and meditation. While I did achieve some success with this, something was still missing. Those practices seemed to calm my spirit, however, when I reentered the real world, the benefits of prayer and meditation seemed to evaporate in the cold hard glare of reality. That's when I begin to physically search for something, anything that could get my fingers humming over my computer keyboard again.

That's when I found it: My PhD dissertation, written years ago. How I stumbled on it, I don't know. Somehow it seemed to make its way from wherever I had it stashed to the top of my to-do pile on my desk. As I held it in my hand, I didn't know what to think.

At first, as I read, it intrigued me. I realized I missed the person who wrote it. She seemed so self assured. I enjoyed the way she used language. Hope permeated each phrase.

That's when I realized that document could possibly hold the key I was looking for to help me in my current situation, the one that could break the self defeating pattern I had somehow fallen into.

The main topic of that dissertation was Neuro Linguistic Programming, (NLP for short) and how metaphysical practitioners can use it to better assist their clients. In a nutshell, NLP explores the association (Programming) between language (Linguistic) and our behavior (Neuro).

In re-reading that dissertation, I became transfixed on how patterns shape our lives, society, our world. As I pondered my situation, I realized my inability to create followed a fairly predictable pattern... one that I had perfected through persistent practice.

Here's the pattern as it typically unfolded: I awoke each morning with dread. Then, I trudged through my morning activities declaring dislike for my life. Every new opportunity arrived dripping in terror. I withdrew from the world, avoided everybody, forced myself through each day, dreading the next.

The more I read, the more I realized I was sacrificing each day to a horrible future that hadn't even arrived.

And that pattern affected every facet of my being.
That's when the seeds for this book were planted...

3

THE POCKET POWER PHILOSOPHY

This isn't your average self help book. I'm not going to dole out advice willy-nilly, tell you to change your mindset, then blame you when this new type of thinking doesn't instantly transform everything. Nope. Not going to happen.

I won't ask you to ignore reality, tell you to slap a smile on your face, adjust your attitude, and pretend everything's hunky dori. There's nothing more irritating than when I'm navigating a difficult situation and someone with good intentions informs me that if I would just shift my attitude, cancer would dissolve, relationships would magically heal themselves, and money would float through my windows and landed my pocketbook.

To be honest, none of that is ever happened to me when I was going through my most difficult times. That said, sometimes a good hard look at the reality of any given situation will help you discover truths about yourself you never realized before. Often you'll develop tools to make yourself stronger and more resilient, too.

If there's one thing I know, it's this:

Life isn't always easy.

A good attitude can make difficult situations easier... sometimes... although it's not a magic elixir.

Bad things happen, even when you've behaved. Sometimes calamity strikes when you least expect it. Bad things happen to good people. Sometimes life simply doesn't make sense.

However, life is still wonderful, a privilege. Every moment, as clichéd as it sounds, is truly a gift. That said, the less time you spend in despair, the faster you can get onto this wonderful thing we call "life."

So here's the deal: the Pocket Power philosophy begins with a firm grasp on reality, the good and bad, the ups and downs, the black and whites and every color in between. It's all good because it's all reality.

However, you don't dwell on the stuff you consider "bad" for long because you're about to discover how focused action will often propel your current situation to a different, more agreeable place. Better yet, if you put some thought into that "more agreeable" place, you can actually find yourself advancing towards your ultimate goal faster than you ever thought possible. (If you haven't thought about your ultimate goal for quite a while, don't worry. We'll cover that in great detail in just a minute.)

Whether your ultimate goal includes something like better health, financial freedom, gold star relationships, you name it... knowing exactly what you want... your ultimate goal... you need a roadmap to get there. That's where Pocket Power comes in.

Pocket Power is not only a compact book, it's an easy to utilize strategy guide that allows to not only embrace reality, but to change it. For good.

Before I close this section we need to discuss a topic that's near and dear to my heart.

If you've read any of my other titles, you know I talk a lot about the topic of Polaris. You probably haven't given Polaris a second thought for quite a while. That's about to change. Here's the deal on that:

I'm a Minnesotan. Growing up in the northland, Polaris, the north star, has always been a big part of my life. We discussed it in elementary school. We located it every time it got dark enough to star surf.

I always dreamed about the sailors who navigated their way to the New World, always using Polaris as their guide.

Growing up, it was drilled into my psyche that no matter where you are in the northern hemisphere, if you can find Polaris, you can find your way home.

I always think about Polaris when I consider my ultimate goal, the one thing I want to accomplish in this lifetime. And now that I've wrestled cancer, my Polaris has become even more important.

Now... don't assume that because you may not have had a life defining moment... yet... that you can't find your Polaris.

The crazy thing is this:

You already know what your Polaris is. It's whispered in your ear since the day you were born. It's that quiet voice complaining every time you take even one step away from your ultimate dream, your life purpose, your highest goal.

The problem is society, common sense, upbringing, any number of factors easily squelch that delicate, persistent voice until after a while, it transforms into despair, hopelessness, the acceptance of a seemingly inescapable rut grinding you through every waking moment.

Sadly, most people live lives in quiet despair, having given up on the possibility of a joyous life, every day taking one step closer to that ultimate realization of their true life purpose.

But, if you're reading this book, you've acknowledged there's more to life than earning a wage. You've felt the spark of Polaris ignite your true desires and you're ready to take action, throw aside mediocrity, and demand excellence from your time and effort.

To help you, I've distilled everything you need into this short volume. I know your time is valuable. I don't have even one minute for filler. After all, time is a finite resource, one of the few that is truly nonrenewable. That makes it your most precious commodity. My vow is to never waste your time while providing you with the instantly useful tools to not only help you identify your Polaris, but to help you advance towards it in record time.

That, in a nutshell, is the Pocket Power philosophy.

Are you ready to get started? It's time to allow your Polaris to guide you home...

4

P IS FOR POW

It was true love. They met online and before you could say "Plenty of Fish," she was engaged.

He was so charming, nobody cared for her more than he did. His attentive texts guided her through some truly thorny situations. She knew they were soulmates.

When they finally met in person, he was too good to be true. His kindness felt magnified a hundredfold every time she looked into his eyes. After a whirlwind romance, they married. That's when everything changed.

The cycle begin on day one of their marriage. She would do something fairly innocuous, perhaps ask him to pick up a few of his messes, he would explode. His mood swings grew wider as the years progressed.

Trying to recapture the magic of their online dating, she persevered, attempting to become the perfect person he desired. Unfortunately, nothing she did could trigger his happiness.

After a number of years of marriage, she realized she had somehow entered a never ending cycle of dealing with his anger, disappointment, demeaning behavior. Meanwhile she attempted perfection, a cheerleading attitude, smoothing over his barbed insults towards others.

After a particularly hurtful conversation concerning his infidelity (as well as his blaming her for his dalliances), she finally found her breaking point. She decided then and there to leave.

She broke the pattern. She shattered the cycle.

IF YOU RECALL, just a few moments ago, we talked about patterns. Let's review and expand on it a little:

Everything you do has basically been patternized. Your morning routine, that's a pattern. The way you get dressed, another pattern. Your work routine... yup, a pattern.

Patterns aren't a good thing or a bad thing. They're simply a shortcut way of doing things without having to rethink it every single time. Without patterns, it would take a lot longer for you to perform routine tasks.

Patterns make our life smoother until they don't.

Here's an example: Cross your arms. Now, try to cross them backwards. You'll quickly discover you have to put a fair amount of thought into changing that particular pattern.

If crossing your arms backwards requires thought, imagine how breaking larger patterns can challenge your inner self.

So, the first step in reclaiming your Polaris, is recognizing patterns that undermine your ultimate goal, interrupting them, and then building new patterns.

But, before I get too far into this, let me tell you where we're headed.

I've taken the word "Power" (as in Pocket Power) and

turned it into an acronym. That means each letter in the word "Power" stands for a technique you'll perform... an ability you'll master, that will help interrupt patterns that don't serve you anymore and help you build new patterns that will propel you towards your Polaris.

I use the acronym POWER because it's easy for you to remember, simple to implement, and can be completed within 30 seconds.

So, when you find yourself deep in a pattern that doesn't serve you, all you have to remember is the word "Power" and you have every tool you need to break the cycle and plant your feet firmly on the path towards your ultimate goal.

Cool, eh?

Let's start with the first letter, "P". Judging from the title of this chapter I'm sure you can figure out what it stands for. Now, I'll explain how to use the first tool in your Pocket Power arsenal.

The letter "P" stands for POW. This first step is so important that I intentionally used the first three letters in the word "POWer" because I want to make it super simple to remember.

Here's how it works.

When you find yourself repeating a pattern you no longer want to repeat, do what NLP practitioners call a "Pattern Interrupt." A Pattern Interrupt is like a small explosion... a POW that interrupts (duh) a less than useful pattern and jars your reality just a little.

This pattern interrupt can be almost anything.

Here's an example: I once knew a child who, when they didn't get a toy they desired, would drop to the floor and engage in a full on temper tantrum. This would cause adults surrounding the child to scramble, attempting to placate her. Because she often did this in public, she usually wound up either receiving the item that triggered the tantrum or would wail throughout the entire store causing strangers to toss disparaging glances our way.

This was a pattern this child engaged in for very long time because it worked well for her. Then, she met me.

I happen to be someone who doesn't appreciate noise or embarrassment. So, when we visited the local discount store and she began winding up into her pattern, I knew I had to act fast.

As we strolled past the toy department, she demanded her item. I kept walking. She inhaled, preparing to scream. That's when I turned towards her and said, "Did you notice that humongous booger on your face? We should probably get rid of it before someone teases you about it."

Her mouth dropped open. Her hand flew to her face. Then she scrambled towards the bathroom.

Crisis averted. Pattern interrupted.

Now, I'm fully aware I engaged in an untruth. But, because of my white lie, the two of us were able to enjoy our shopping trip.

Also, be aware that that particular pattern interrupt may or or may not work in your situation. The point is, it's important to break that pattern.

Pattern interrupts can include anything from a ridiculous statement, a loud noise, a change of routine... anything will work as long as it interrupts the undesired thought... thus the behavior.

I once knew an NLP practitioner who routinely instructed his clients to stand, throw their arms above their head, and yell "Woop" when they wanted to change their emotional state and/or break a pattern.

In your case, just remember the word POW. Then attach a pattern interrupt to that word. If you're at a loss for ideas, just check out the Pocket Power Toolbox at the end of this book. That's where you'll find a nice list of ideas for pattern interrupts.

The most important thing to remember is, when you find yourself in a self-defeating pattern, if you recognize your behavior won't propel you towards your Polaris, if you find yourself in an emotional state that doesn't suit you, immediately cease the behavior, perform your POW, then get yourself back on track.

Here's another example: I've dealt with cancer. When I find myself thinking it isn't worth launching a new long-term project because I'll likely die early, I engage my POW.

I interrupt those self-defeating thoughts by yelling (really loud) "Yee Haw!" After doing so, I sound so ridiculous that I'm generally smiling at that point. Then, I remind myself that many people have lived years after that diagnosis. I also tell myself I could easily be one of them. Then, I get back to work.

POWing the patterns that don't serve you is an incredible start towards achieving your ultimate goal. It's a simple technique, but never underestimate its power.

Once you've POWed a less than useful pattern, then you can move onto the next letter in our acronym. Wait 'til you see how easy that one is...

5

O IS FOR OWN YOUR TIME

"One phone call can derail an entire day," I whined, "I don't understand why they won't just leave me alone..."

The number of times I've said that is likely too embarrassing to recount.

But, here's the deal:

Nobody can take advantage of your time unless you let them. And it wasn't until I understood and embraced this concept that I finally was able to progress towards my goals.

Understanding that time is a truly finite resource, it's the one great equalizer every being on this planet has in common. No matter who you are, what you do, the number of your possessions, your bank account statistics... the one thing every human shares is that we all possess the exact same 24 hours each day. No matter how we try, we cannot increase or decrease that number.

Understanding how precious your time is, that's the first acknowledgement you must face before you can move onto the next step in your POWER Process. This is because once you've POWed and interrupted a self-defeating pattern, your next step, the O in POWER, is to Own Your Time.

Of course, the ownership of anything involves understanding that you, and you alone, are responsible for the care of that concept.

If you "own" a dog, you're responsible for tending to it, feeding, grooming, veterinary care, you cannot assume anyone else will rise to the occasion. If you own a car, you can't expect anybody else to fill it with gasoline, keep it tidy, maintain the engine.

And considering time is a nonrenewable resource, imagine how much more valuable it is than a machine that can be replaced with a trip to the local dealership.

When you realize you are the caretaker of your time, you begin to treat it with a little more respect.

You realize you need to be mindful of any new opportunity that comes your way and carefully weigh it, always evaluating whether it will propel you closer to your Polaris versus whether it has the real potential to become a time wasting rabbit hole.

Here's an example: I'm a writer. Every now and then, I'm presented with an opportunity to join a mastermind that promises interaction with some pretty big names in my community. Often for hefty price, of course.

Unfortunately, more than once I've joined a group thinking, "This could be something quite useful in helping me grow my audience."

Sadly, that's not generally how it works.

In two of the masterminds I've joined, both appeared to have benefited the organizers far more than the participants. That's not necessarily a bad thing if my goal was to help others. But my goal was to grow my business. Therefore, my greatest regret in both those cases was the time I lost on side projects, business trips, phone calls, spinning my wheels... I fear that precious time was lost forever.

I've discovered, that when I find myself in the throes of excitement, when bombarded with new ideas, I have the type of personality that appears to be prone towards exploring rabbit holes.

Instead of sticking to my writing schedule and engaging in focused research on new topics, I often find myself chatting online looking for new ideas, trawling Facebook to research new marketing trends, interviewing potential collaborators, and getting swept into an emotional tsunami whenever Amazon (or a similar bookstore) "wronged" a fellow author.

Now, don't get me wrong. These are all honorable activities (for the most part). Unfortunately, most of them don't fit into my lifestyle, they certainly don't propel me towards my Polaris, and they usually distracted me from my important daily tasks.

I quickly realized how many seemingly awesome opportunities didn't fit my priorities, once I broke the pattern of immediately assuming somebody outside myself understood my Polaris better than I did. That's when I was able to take ownership of my time, politely decline invitations, and resume my enjoyable, sane writing career.

When practicing Owning Your Time, one of the greatest skills you can develop is the ability to say, "no."

At first, it can be difficult, especially when you have to decline requests from people you care about. It's also difficult to turn down educational "opportunities" from smart marketers. New courses pop up all the time. They're time sucks. If you truly need to learn something new, carefully evaluate before you fork over copious dough on a scheme that will not only set you back monetarily, but can cramp your schedule.

I'm a naturally helpful person so nurturing the skill of Owning my Time... saying "no"... felt so very foreign and was initially quite difficult to execute.

Here are a few tricks I learned along the way to make the process easier:

1. When someone calls and asks for assistance, always pause before you reply. This gives you time to think. Try to give yourself 24 hours before deciding on a plan of action. If you're presented with an opportunity and must make an instant decision, that instant decision is always "no." Marketers like to conjure scarcity, it boosts response. If they can't wait for 24 hours, they don't need your money.

2. If someone has asked for your assistance, or if a new opportunity has presented itself, discuss it with a trusted friend, preferably somebody who is aware of your Polaris and can give an outside opinion. If a peer wants to work with you, Google a bit to find out what other people in your field are saying.

3. Lastly, and this is probably more important than anything else, take a moment to sit in solitude. Imagine your life as it is right now versus what it could become if you follow through on this opportunity. Try to imagine how you could change as a person if you affiliate with these people. If you like what you see, give it a whirl. If this task and/or opportunity in any way seeks to change who you are or (worse yet) appears to disrespect your Polaris, it's imperative to decline.

In my mastermind example, I discovered, to my chagrin, that most of the people affiliated with that group appeared to value sales over quality. That core value colored every piece of advice I received from them and ran contrary to everything I'd built into Filbert Publishing. In the end, I felt as though my time would have been better spent doing what I do best: write, publish, and market.

If you've decided not to take part in that particular request, now it's time to guard your boundaries while tactfully declining. There are number of ways to do this.

1. You can simply say "no." No explanation necessary. It's amazing how those tiny two letters can free you from many hours of spinning your wheels. If the other person persists, just remember you're under no obligation to explain. But if you feel you must...

2. A simple, "I wish I could, but I can't" or "It won't fit into my schedule," often works wonders. Very few people will persist at this point. But if they do, simply repeat, "No."

3. Remember, the fewer words you use, the less ammunition the person trying to persuade you will receive. Keep it simple. Remember you don't owe anybody an explanation.

Your Polaris is precious and treat it as such.

Fast recap: Once you've interrupted patterns that do not propel you toward your Polaris, your next task is to Own Your Time. After that, things get very interesting...

6

W IS FOR WIN THE MINDSET GAME

Way back when, Filbert Publishing published a monthly newsletter titled, "The Creative Mindset." It was a wonderful experience, one that I cherish to this day. Since then, it appears as though the concept of "Mindset" has become clouded. I hope to correct this right now.

Ever since a certain new age documentary hit the airwaves, I have felt an annoying, yet persistent call to be unrelentingly positive.

I cringe when I view my Facebook page, with cardboard positivity dripping from far too many posts, with nearly everybody living perfect lives, smiles on every face, it's getting difficult to unbraid fiction from reality. It's sometimes annoying to watch that scrolling fiction day after day and feel as though my life is completely up to par.

Truth is, I had cancer. And despite my league of Facebook friends proclaiming I've "got this," calling me a "cancer warrior," truth is, I could get it again. In fact, I didn't triumph, I pretty much whined through the whole experience. I gained weight. I've had copious cancer scares since then. A lot of cancer cr*p is downright difficult. And I didn't post about it on Facebook because to do so would expose my imperfections alongside carefully constructed non-realities.

My point? (You know I've got one...)

Thinking happy thoughts is a fine and dandy activity. Sometimes it'll do you good.

Conversely, thinking unhappy thoughts can be a fine and dandy activity, too. Sometimes it'll do you good.

However, ignoring reality, not acknowledging every shade of color from the moody darks to the perky lights, will likely make you more of a robot than a human.

It's in embracing the entire range of human emotions from dark to light, truly accepting reality in all its imperfect glory... that's where the sweet spot resides.

One of the bright spots in my Facebook feed was Tom. He was an awesome person. He also had terminal colon cancer. He knew he was going to die. Yet, he continued to post his reality from the scars that zig zagged his abdomen to his skeletal frame as he lived the "cannonball life," jumping into fellow colon cancer friend's swimming pools as he traveled across the USA.

He shared every facet of his journey, every triumph, every failure. While he received tremendous support, there was always a kind reader who reminded him that if he simply wouldn't acknowledge his upcoming death, he could probably extend his life ("science proves this!").

I'm not sure how anybody could write that to a dying person. Perhaps they felt they were helping. Perhaps watching him live so close to death made them feel vulnerable. I honestly couldn't say.

However, when confronted about her actions, she defended herself by saying this:

"Everybody knows that if you look at something while driving, chances are good you'll hit it. That's why it's important to not look at anything you do not want. If you don't want to get sick, don't look at sickness. If you don't want to be poor, don't look at poor people."

I gasped when I read her response. First, while it may be true that it's important to keep your eye on your goal, she took that truth, divided it in half, and mixed it with a large pile of crap.

To tell anybody it's important to ignore the sick, the poor, the weak... that's just absurd, not to mention cruel. However, it illustrates my point.

Life isn't perfect. To deny imperfections exist in order to maintain your sunny (yet delusional) disposition is not only selfish, it's ineffective, inhuman, and cruel.

So, what, exactly, is this winning mindset you need to develop in order to fulfill the "W" in POWER?

A winning mindset is always aware of your Polaris. It knows you'll eventually get there if you stay the course, remain focused, and can elegantly interrupt behaviors that don't serve you.

A winning mindset also acknowledges reality. It knows you will not win every single time. It does know, however, that you'll learn something every single time you fail.

A winning mindset treats other people with respect. However, it isn't relentlessly positive. A winning mindset allows you to cry, laugh, feel bummed, enjoy buoyant ecstasy... the entire rainbow of emotions.

A winning mindset doesn't dwell on the negative or the positive. It enjoys life when it's appropriate, it mourns when it needs to, and it knows that's okay. It's healthy. It allows you to be the human you are.

A winning mindset throws out all masks. If the people

around you have difficulty accepting your sadness, that's their problem. If you're bummed, feel free to grouse a bit. If you're having a great day you feel free to smile, but it's never forced for the sole purpose of trying to gain the favor of some invisible power.

A winning mindset embraces reality and understands that every new day is truly a gift that not everyone of us will experience.

Because time is precious. It's nonrenewable. Nor is it a guarantee.

So, Fast review (BTW, I'm pleased you made it this far!)

P = POW. Interrupt patterns that don't serve you.

O = Own Your Time.

W = Win the Mindset Game

Next up? E. Guess what that stands for... (Don't worry, we'll put this all together in a bit.)

7

E IS FOR EMPATHY

It's frustrating to live for many years knowing your Polaris is simmering away on the back burner, languishing, waiting for you to proceed forward. To make matters worse, many people with an artistic bent can feel their talent rising within them, begging for release, causing much frustration.

At the most inopportune time... during a meeting, while driving, eating your lunch, listening to coworkers bicker and gossip, without warning, a voice within you says, "Is this all there is? Is this how you're going to spend your life? What ever happened to [insert your dream]?"

Worse yet, while watching a movie, enjoying a concert, reading a book, meandering through an art museum, driving past a vast forest, cheering a sports team... that same small voice often whispers, "You could do that. Why aren't you doing that? That's what you always wanted to do..."

Hopefully, none of these scenarios describes you. But if it does, don't despair.

I once read that most people live their lives in a state of quiet desperation. It's weird to think about the number of unfulfilled destinies (and sad dreams) that lie beneath the millions of tombstones peppering the landscape.

The truth is, I personally know very few people who actually have the time, resources, or information they need to truly live the life they know they should lead.

I'm not going to focus on finances at this point, that comes later. Right now, I'm discussing spiritual issues, mortality and the ability to not only advance towards your Polaris, but to actually achieve that goal... live your destiny... know with all your heart, if you were to die today, you'd pass on knowing you've fulfilled your purpose.

And you can start doing that at this exact moment. Plus, it's free. Doesn't cost a dime.

You see, life can get cluttered. Sometimes it's overwhelming to not only face another day, but the prospect of adding anything extra feels crushing. This is the exact point where good decision making, delegating, trusting, and persistence pays off.

There are billions of people on this planet, each person with a personal agenda. When someone asks you to assist them in some way, when you're invited to join a particular group, it's easy for them to see how your presence can become a benefit to them. However, before you take one step forward, you need to decide how their presence in your life will benefit you as well as your ultimate goal... your Polaris.

It's always wise to remember every person in your life has the inalienable right to ask you for anything. At the same time, it's exceedingly important to remember you have every right to use the word, "no."

But, let's talk about that for just a minute.

When you find yourself in the position to decline a situation that won't complement your ultimate goal, sometimes it's easy to rationalize a reason to "help" the other person.

"No one else can do this."

"They really need my help."

"I can squeeze this project/them into my schedule."

But beware. That may not be the case. Multiple small commitments can add up to huge time sucks.

Before you feel bad about declining a request, this is when you have to be particularly conscious about employing the "E" in your POWER exercise: Empathy.

Empathy is defined as the ability to understand and share the feelings of others. Let's tear it apart a little.

It's important to understand that 99% of the people you encounter possess their own agenda, goals, their personal Polaris. This is neither good or bad, it's merely reality.

Interacting with other people is often a dance, each person searching for ways to advance their own goals. Again, this isn't good or bad, it's merely reality.

As a person who possesses their own Polaris as well as a POWER practice, this gives you a unique ability to approach each new interaction as an outsider observing the proceedings. This gives you an edge when it comes to evaluating each new opportunity as well as deciding whether or not it is a good fit with your Polaris.

Here's an example: I mentioned earlier I was a member of a mastermind group containing a full compliment of very successful, powerful people in my field. When I received the invitation, I was floored, so flattered I could barely see straight.

Red flag number one: Flattery.

But, then I paused. Knowing that the first step in any high-powered persuasion technique is to stir the emotions (always beware... if you feel your emotions arise, always take one step back and be super cautious before you proceed) I decided to take my time before I made a decision.

They replied, "Your invitation is good for 24 hours. After that, you'll forfeit your seat at the table and it'll be offered to somebody else."

Red flag number two: if anyone rushes you towards your decision, that generally isn't a good thing. Manufactured scarcity sells well, however it doesn't always serve well.

I breathed deep. My first instinct was to hop on board. But then I engaged my POWER.

POW: I broke my cycle of jumping on board without thinking.

O: I owned my time by calculating how much time I'd spend on the mastermind discussion board, answering Facebook questions, traveling across the country... you get the drift.

W: My mindset felt perplexed. It's scary to work alone, I wasn't sure I have the chops to proceed forward even though I done exactly that for over a decade. That was about the time I realized just how powerful their sales presentation was.

E: I'm not one to burn bridges. I knew there were some wonderful people in this mastermind. I understood they may have actually needed a fast answer, they weren't necessarily being pushy. However, that communication style didn't fit my personality. So, while constructing my reply, I made a mental note to be as professional, kind, yet firm as possible. Plus, I was positive there had to be someone who would benefit from being a member of that particular group and I didn't want to deny them their chance.

I didn't join that mastermind, even though it was apparently the "one missing piece that would guarantee success beyond my wildest dreams for the rest of my life."

Turns out, the sensation of advancing towards my Polaris, not getting distracted by moneymaking schemes, gave me more joy than meeting some of the most (so called) powerful people in my industry.

How are you faring? Have you played with your new POWER tool?

Let's review because every time you read this, a little more of it sinks into your psyche and very soon, the process will become as natural as breathing:

P: POW — break your less than useful pattern.

O: Own your time.

W: Win the mindset game.

E: Empathy, gain a little understanding of the other people around you. This helps you decide whether or not, in a very nonjudgmental way, if you will be a good fit in working together.

Are you ready for the final piece of the POWER puzzle? That's coming next as well as some tools and info on how to put everything together in an elegant, effective way.

8

R IS FOR REVIEW AND RELAX

If you've made it this far. Wow... you're amazing. Pat yourself on the back.

I've been publishing books since 2001 and can state without reservation that 95% of most readers don't get this far. You truly must be an extraordinary person.

To be honest, you've already done most of the hard lifting because this step is a cake walk in comparison to everything you've accomplished so far.

Let's see where we're at:

First, you've identified your Polaris. If you haven't done so yet, you're likely well on your way to embracing your ultimate goal. Just as a reminder, you already know what it is, it's been tucked inside your soul, silently waiting for you to acknowledge it, for as long as you've been alive.

Then, thanks to your new POWER practice when you identify a behavior or opportunity that doesn't support your ultimate goal (your Polaris), you've devised a way to interrupt... POW... that pattern and give yourself the time to develop new habits, new ways of thinking that will propel you towards your Polaris.

You've learned how to OWN your time. You know each moment is your most precious resource because time is nonrenewable. Once you allow even one minute to slip through your fingers, it's gone. You know every human being on earth is 100% equal in this regard. Everyone of us has the same 24 hours each day. How we decide to invest that time is completely up to us (for the most part).

You know that a WINNING MINDSET accepts reality. You aren't a pie-in-the-sky thinker, someone who sits in the easy chair thinking happy thoughts, waiting for opportunity to float through the nearby window. You know good things happen to people as well as bad. And that's okay, because that's reality. That said, you also acknowledge current reality can change and a good attitude is usually advantageous.

E stands for EMPATHY. Sometimes the world is a harsh place. But when you're proceeding toward your Polaris, you've discovered you have a sense of peace, hope, a stillness that surpasses all understanding. And in light of this new way of being, you can understand that the actions of others are often driven by their own agendas. You also understand you will always strive to treat everybody with a level of respect.

And as your final step, we will now discuss the letter R.

The "R" in your POWER practice stands for "REVIEW AND RELAX."

Ah... doesn't that feel good? I love relaxing. The reviewing part isn't that bad either.

This is how it works:

The POWER process can take place in a relatively short period of time. You POW and interrupt your thought process and/or behavior. Then you proceed with the other steps. In this final moment after your decision is made and you've executed it, now's the time to take a moment and evaluate (review) how everything went.

Did both parties part ways amicably?

What could you have done better?

What part of your interaction felt really good?

What is an action you will definitely repeat?

What action will you avoid next time?

Was your pattern interrupt effective?

How well did you defend your boundaries and/or own your time?

What does your mindset feel like right now?

What does your body feel like?

Describe your breathing.

What is your state of being?

Were you able to express empathy during the interaction? Did you actually feel empathy?

If you have time, replay the interaction in your mind and watch it like an impartial observer. Take notes if you need to, highlighting interesting points.

Then, after you have reviewed the interaction, pat yourself on the back, make notes on how you'll proceed differently next time, and relax. Take a moment to feel good. You just did something incredibly huge.

You defended your Polaris. You created boundaries. And believe it or not, as time progresses, you'll discover those around you will respect you more.

Better yet, you won't feel rudderless anymore. You'll create goals and actually follow through. You'll awaken each morning with a glimmer of hope in your heart.

You'll feel empowered because you are empowered.

You've claimed your dream and now have every tool you need to venture forth on the path only you can walk.

As you relax, you'll realize you always held this power. And as you reflect, you'll realize you'll never want to give it away again.

Because it feels awesome.

9

PUTTING IT ALL TOGETHER

The POWER system is deceptively simple and incredibly powerful. It cuts through extraneous crap faster than anything else I've ever tried. It's not pie-in-the-sky nor is it packed full of woo. It's an incredibly useful, reality based method of keeping your eye on Polaris while politely bypassing anything that can throw you off track.

Better yet, if you find yourself on the wrong path, using the POWER steps, you can easily find your way back. That's pretty cool.

Let's see how this looks in real life.

I was working with a Filbert Publishing author who wanted to write a sequel to her nonfiction title. Before she began writing, I asked her, "What is your ultimate goal?"

She had no idea what I was talking about. So I spoke with her about Polaris, her ultimate goal... the reason she's alive. As we spoke, I couldn't help but notice a hitch in her throat as she spoke.

"I never dare think about it," she whispered, "do you

actually believe anyone can achieve something like that? I mean... live my dream. It sounds trite."

"Of course. I believe anyone can advance towards their Polaris," I replied, "you'd be amazed at some of the things I've seen. When you actively work toward your ultimate goal, the magic is amazing."

I didn't hear a sound from the other side of the line for a while. Finally she spoke. "Stories. I've always wanted to tell stories. But I never believed I could make a living doing that."

Then, I asked her what she'd need to do to start progressing towards that goal. It wasn't an easy conversation, True honesty is rarely simple. However, as we spoke, as if magic, pieces started falling into place.

"I throw away a lot of time," she said.

"Can you elaborate?"

"Chores," she said, "House stuff. But I just realized my husband's a grown up. He can take care of..." She listed a few family tasks.

"That'll free up some time," I said.

"I'm done teaching Sunday school. It's not just the Sunday stuff, the preparation is killing me. I have to shop, plan, go to meetings. I never liked it, never will. They'll have to get along without me."

By now, she was on a roll.

"I'm not taking on any extra shifts at the hospital. This isn't my dream job. I'm going to take that time to write."

And she made some tougher decisions.

"I'm getting up an hour early. I'm going to do 15 minutes of yoga followed by 45 minutes of uninterrupted writing."

And so she continued. Before we finished the call, she had a solid plan in place. Then I asked the really tough question, "How will you defend your plan?"

That's what she got introduced to POWER.

We both knew she would initially receive some resistance to her plan. "I know you love your family," I said, "but, what are you going to do when they resist their new tasks?"

"In the past," she said, "I'd feel sorry for them and go ahead and do it myself."

"That's a pattern. One that won't work anymore. You need to develop a new pattern."

So... she decided when someone approached her, assuming their excuse would cause her to complete the task herself, she would immediately, and without thinking, break the cycle. She decided to accomplish this by laughing, preferably as loud as she could.

"How will you own your time?" I asked.

"I plan on laughing really loud and follow up by saying something to the effect of, 'Nice try. You're a grown-up. I have things to do, too.'"

"And your mindset?"

"I plan on looking at this as a way for other members of my family to grow up, mature, become productive members of society."

"That's definitely a winning mindset," I said, "And your empathy?"

"Of course, I understand how they feel. I'd love to have my own personal assistant, too. But, I've served my family for many years. It's my turn. I'm sure they'll understand."

"Sounds great," I said, "I can't wait to hear how it all turns out."

And that's how it was left until I talked to her the following week.

"How did it go," I asked.

She looked like a changed woman. Her eyes were bright, she exuded confidence.

"It was amazing," she said. "I don't feel like I'm in a rut anymore."

"Details," I said, "I need details."

She laughed. "The family was pretty surprised at first. I told them I was going to make time every day to write. They were fine with it until I told them they had to pick up the slack."

"And?"

"It was okay for the first couple days. Then, I noticed things were slipping, chores were getting left undone. The house started to go downhill."

"What did you do?"

"I almost jumped in to take care of everything. Then I realized I was dealing with a pattern that wouldn't serve me anymore. I decided to engage the POWER practice that we've been working on."

"Sounds exciting!"

"It was!"

"Tell me about it!"

"Well," she said, "I knew I had to interrupt the pattern... POW it. So, for some reason... and I'm not sure how I picked this... but I started singing Yellow Submarine at the top of my lungs. My son thought I was crazy. But, it broke the moment."

She continued, "Then when he was feeling perplexed, I explained I was now a writer and he had to complete his chores. I reminded him he agreed to do so." Then she laughed. "I'm not sure why I did this, but I told him I could either clean or prepare supper, which just happened to be my chore that day." She added, "I guess he wanted to eat..."

"That wasn't excellent way to OWN YOUR TIME."

"My WINNING MINDSET was strong, too. I had every

confidence that everything would work out. Plus I showed him EMPATHY... I was kind, yet firm."

"Did you REVIEW and RELAX?"

"Absolutely. I knew it wasn't a big deal, but it felt huge to me. I felt fantastic. I like to think he felt a little more independent, too."

I said, "That's what's cool about the POWER practice... everybody seems to win in one way or another."

Best of all? She's still working on more nonfiction titles as a way to keep her income steady. She figures she'll quit working at the hospital soon and will write full time. She also devotes a little time each day to create fiction... her true dream.

It's amazing how quickly the POWER practice can not only achieve results, but can be executed in just a few minutes. When you don't have time to waste, it's nice to utilize techniques that work fast.

Better yet, the feeling of empowerment fuels your ambitions and propels them forward faster than you ever could've imagined. Rather than losing days to inertia, indecision, frustration, and resistance... now you have a simple tool that's not only effective, it's transformative.

Are you ready to give it a whirl (if you already haven't)?

Next up: more concrete tools to supercharge your POWER practice.

10

TOOLBOX TO TRANSFORM YOUR LIFE

The POWER practice is elegant in its simplicity. You don't have to have a million tools to make it work. In fact, the simpler you keep the process the more apt you will be too use it.

That said, I'm going to tear the POWER process apart one last time for the sole purpose of giving you some concrete techniques, ideas, tools to make your practice even easier. I'm going to throw quite a few ideas your way. All you have to do is select the strategy that feels like a good fit and run with it. Occasionally reference back to this chapter so you can expand your practice, sharpen your tools, and gain the ability to joyfully play with the process.

Here we go.

Step 1: POW

If you recall, your first step is to interrupt self-defeating patterns. As you look around, once your eyes are opened, you'll discover a myriad of patterns surrounding you.

Many years ago, I had the privilege of meeting a man known as the "Wizard of San Juan," A.K.A. Dr. Dave Dobson. A renowned NLP practitioner, stories of his ability to induct hypnosis was legendary.

When I finally met Dr. Dave, I wasn't sure what to expect. However meeting an old man wearing pajamas surrounded by breathing apparatus wasn't on my list. But, there he was.

I sat in the little audience, curious, watching this man in action. Anyone remotely affiliated with NLP (at the time, I was a mere newbie) buzzed with excitement. Finally, one participant called out, "What is the best way to induce a trance state?"

Dobson stared at the man for quite a while. He did that a lot... staring at someone before he spoke. I didn't understand what he was doing but a hush fell over the room as his eyes bore into the man. Finally, he took a long, deep breath, and intoned, "That's the problem, isn't it?" Long pause. "People just don't understand." Longer pause. "It's not a matter of inducing a trance." His eyes slowly swept the room, focusing on each person in front of him... including me. "It's a matter of getting people out of the trance they're already in."

Then, he took a long swig of water. Meanwhile, my mind was officially blown realizing he just done it; he'd changed the trance state of every single person in that room.

And, that's what you're dealing with... interrupting long held patterns (which are basically trance states).

You can interrupt your state (or another person's state/pattern) by:

* Doing something unexpected.
* An unusual sound.

* Say something odd.
* Silence.
* Laugh.
* Drastically change a topic.
* Engage in some exercise.
* Stretch and yawn loudly.
* Grab a cup of coffee.
* Anything that breaks the pattern and changes focus will work.

These are just a few options, have fun. As Ms. Frizzle in The Magic School Bus would say, "Take chances. Make mistakes. Get messy."

Step 2: Own Your Time:

This one's easy. All you have to do is reclaim what is already yours: your time. Some techniques include:

* Say "no."
* "I wish I could, but I can't."
* "That doesn't fit in my schedule."
* "Sounds interesting, but no."
* "That sounds like a great project for you. I hope you enjoy it.
* I'll be rooting for you."
* "My focus has shifted and this doesn't fit in my plans."
* "I can't wait to see how this turns out for you. Have fun!"

Step 3: Your Winning Mindset:

I've discovered that mindset is like a muscle, the more you exercise it, the stronger it becomes. I'm not looking for persistent positivity. However, it's always good to acknowledge a positive mindset sometimes allows you to see options you otherwise could have missed. But to force a sunny disposition on yourself is just silly.

So, your assignment is to learn to ride the fine line between reality and hope. I've discovered hope is far easier to cultivate when I'm advancing towards my Polaris. I think you'll discover the same phenomenon.

In the beginning, when this process appears to be the most difficult, it's helpful to engage in some of these activities:

* No matter how busy you are, do one thing every day toward your Polaris... even if you can only spend a minute or two on it. That short amount of time will plant seeds of hope that can sustain your dream.

* Actively search for ways to cultivate your dream. Read books that support your Polaris. Visit appropriate websites.

* Actively search out a time wasters... mindless web searching, endless social media conversations, black hole comment threads... eliminate them and use that time to build your path towards your Polaris. Doing this will nurture your mindset.

Step 4: Cultivate Empathy:

If you walk a mile in someone else's shoes, you will better understand them.

It's hard not to notice that the world has become a little less friendly. Let's not be one of those people.

As you place yourself in other people's situations, as you understand that they are also dealing with their own issues, their place in the universe, heck, sometimes they just have to get stuff done... it makes this process much easier when you realize that simply because someone else's Polaris doesn't align with yours, that doesn't make them a bad person, pushy, perhaps even irritating.

Always remember, anyone has the right to ask for your assistance or participation. There's no harm in asking. You also have every right to decline without repercussions.

As you advanced towards your Polaris you will surely encounter people on the way towards their own ultimate goal. If their aims align with yours... by all means enjoy the ride with them. If it so happens at their Polaris doesn't fit well with your goals, you are more than free to send them on their way with your blessing.

Here are some tips:

* Understand most people are so wrapped up in their own lives that any perceived slight on your part is likely incorrect. Generally speaking, when someone lashes out at you, it's nothing personal and says more about them than it does you.

* Not everybody is going to like you. That's okay. Send them towards their own destination with your blessing.

* Treasure people who are kind.

* Remember that trust is earned and proceed forward in any relationship at a pace that feels correct to you.

* It's okay to take your time. If anybody rushes you, feel free to hit the brakes and ponder the situation at your leisure.

STEP 5: Review and Relax:

Sometimes, if you're like me, I can be far harder on myself than any outsider. This is also an easy step to skip. I'd suggest you don't.

It's only in reviewing your actions, along with the other

persons reactions, that you can adjust your course the next time you encounter a pattern you need to break.

Here are few tips:

* Be kind to yourself. If self reflection is a new skill you're just developing, cut yourself a lot of slack. You didn't learn how to walk in a day. I'll bet your bike riding skills were pretty shaky at first. It's the same with self reflection. Many of us were brought up to believe it was important to serve others above yourself. Unfortunately it's very difficult to serve others when you haven't tended to your own needs. And evaluating your interactions and reflecting on those interactions is an important skill. Treated as such.

* Review the situation as an impartial observer. While emotions are important, when you're evaluating a situation, it's important to attempt, as much as possible, to remove emotion so you can better understand the other person's point of view. Doing this also allows you to better identify blind spots in your own reasoning. With every blind spot you identify, you'll gain insight into yourself, discover crazy facets of your personality that you didn't realize existed. You'll understand just how complex and awesome you are.

* Don't forget to relax. This journey towards your Polaris, this adventure of getting to know yourself is the adventure of a lifetime. In fact, it'll take your entire life to unravel this mystery.

And the weirdest part of all? If you're heading towards Polaris... and this is the big secret... you have to realize you'll never arrive. Not one sailor actually made it to Polaris. Not one Boy Scout found his way to that star. But that's not what matters.

What matters is understanding that your journey towards Polaris is the golden grail. It's the adventure that matters. Because it's in that journey towards an unreachable destination that you'll discover the most amazing treasure of all... yourself.

11

THE 30 SECOND CHALLENGE

Here's your cheat sheet. Rip it out of the book... copy and paste it... memorize it (it's short enough to do this), and when you're faced with a less than useful pattern... go for it.

Here's the scenario. You have a goal. You're staring straight into the face of a situation that will not advance you towards your Polaris. The minute you realize it you launch into your POWER practice.

30 Second Scenario #1

Goal: Weight Loss

Location: Grocery Store

Family member: "Hey! Check out these Chocolate Doodles with Extra Nuts! We need to buy some."

You: You have health goals. You know you can't control yourself when it comes to Doodles. Yet, you've lost some weight so why not...

1. POW — You pause before throwing them in the cart.

You breathe deep, taking a moment to feel how loose your pants feel. You like the sensation.

2. OWN YOUR TIME — You reply, "Those look good. But I'm on a roll. My new food plan is going great and I don't want to mess that up. Put those back."

Family member: "But they're good..."

3. WINNING MINDSET — "I know. I've eaten a lot of those. They're ultimately not as fulfilling as a smaller pant size, so no."

Family member: "I suppose..."

4: EMPATHY — "I can see you're disappointed, but how about we go home and do something special together instead... like a bike ride? A walk together? Or we could find a new type of fruit to enjoy."

Family member: "Sure." They get rid of the Doodles."

5: REVIEW AND REFLECT — You keep an eye on your family member, rather surprised how quickly they exchanged a little of your time for an unhealthy treat.

30 Second Scenario #2

Goal: Curb television watching to engage in better time management

You're alone. You just finished dinner. You're a little tired and tempted to sit down and wile away the evening watching television. But you have a Polaris project going.

You flip on the television and are scrolling through viewing options.

1. POW — You pause, realizing how similar and formulaic many of those shows are.

2. OWN YOUR TIME — You realize you could create a much better story.

3. WINNING MINDSET — You tell yourself you're perfectly capable of writing that story.

4. EMPATHY — You acknowledge your fatigue but then compare how you'd feel after spending the night as a couch potato versus how you'll feel after hammering out an outline. You opt for the euphoria of living your dream as a story teller.

5. REFLECT AND REVIEW — You pat yourself on the back because you're now a creator, not a consumer of life.

30 Second Scenario #3

Goal: Clear time to work on a Polaris Project

Person: Hey... can you do BLANK for me?

You want that person to like you so you're about to agree, even though you don't want to.

1. POW — You pause. Think for five seconds. Realize it's not a good fit.

2. OWN YOUR TIME — You reply, "I wish I could, but I can't." You shrug.

Person: But I really need someone to do this for me. You'd be great at it.

3. WINNING MINDSET — "That's flattering, but no. My schedule's packed."

Person: But I really need someone to help.

4. EMPATHY — Pause before speaking. "I know you need help. What about PERSON'S NAME? She'd be a great fit. Plus, this is in her field of interest."

Person: Oh. I may give her a try.

5. REVIEW AND REFLECT — You're thrilled because you defended your Polaris by not filling your schedule with a project that didn't fit well with your ultimate goal.

. . .

Boom. Thirty seconds to freedom. How easy was that?

Once you master the art of implementing pattern interrupts and launch into your POWER practice, the sky's the limit. No goal is too difficult.

Now, plug in some specific situations you've faced into the POWER formula and see how you could alter the outcomes by applying your POWER practice.

You're about to blow your mind...

12

A BONUS!

Let's not say "Goodbye!" I want to hear how you're doing!

If you head to the following link, you can get updates; more hints, tips, and tricks; and be one of the first people to find out when I've got some new (fun) stuff available to supercharge your POWER practice.

If you join us (it's free, for Pete's sake) I've got a special bonus created especially for VIP POWER People. I know you'll love it.

Just surf here:
http://PocketPowerBooks.com
Until then... May you OWN your POWER!

Rudie :)

ABOUT THE AUTHOR

Rudie Jakerson is the author of copious novels under a pen name, a ton of nonfiction, writes marketing materials for entrepreneurs, and generally keeps busy writing. After all, weaving words together in compelling ways, telling thought provoking stories, and helping others has been her Polaris for as long as she can remember.

She's a cancer person and deals with the after affects of that diagnosis every day. On the flip side, her cancer made every moment even more poignant and every year from here on in is truly a gift.

She initially developed the Pocket POWER philosophy while dealing with mindset issues related to her diagnosis. When everything she built collapsed, when she found herself unable to write (her Polaris dimmed!), she wandered through her Shadow of the Valley of Death. It was while sorting through documents, found her PhD dissertation on NLP (Neuro Linguistic Programming). That's when Pocket POWER was born... that's when she found freedom. She started joyfully writing again.

Her hope is that you'll find this process as helpful as it was for her.

Since the completion of this project, Rudie has teamed with a very special partner... a sister with a different mother... who has added incredibly powerful additions to Pocket POWER series. Watch for their collaborations. Better yet, find out what's next on their agenda here:

http://RudieJakerson.com

www.ingramcontent.com/pod-product-compliance
Lightning Source LLC
Chambersburg PA
CBHW060219050426
42446CB00013B/3107